True Connection

Building Meaningful Relationships through Better Communication

Table of Contents

Chapter 1. Introduction

Welcome to a life-changing journey! Our Special Report "True Connection: Building Meaningful Relationships through Better Communication" is an enlightening exploration into the heart of human connections. It's not a technical blueprint, but a heartwarming narrative packed with values, insights, and essential guidelines to open a new era of communication in your life. Developed by leading relationship and communication experts, this report has a friendly tone, real-life examples, and easy-to-follow strategies transforming your interactions into profound bonding experiences. Unlock rich, fulfilling relationships by improving your communication with this engaging read- a purchase you will treasure every day of your life!

Chapter 2. Understanding the Essence of True Connection

Human beings are complex, social creatures. We thrive in the company of others, seeking companionship, empathy, and understanding. At the heart of these interactions is communication - a unique thread that binds us all together. But what is truly necessary for a precise and deep connection? How does one break down barriers, overcome miscommunication, and build meaningful bonds forged out of mutual respect and trust? To answer these questions, we delve into the essence of true connection.

2.1. The Nature of Connection

The concept of connection goes beyond mere conversation and interaction. Imagine you're in a room full of people. You laugh, converse, even share a dance or two. Yet, amidst all this, you still feel lonely. This loneliness amid crowds is a classic symptom of lack of true connection. While you might be surrounded by warm bodies, the absence of an emotional bond makes you feel isolated, detached.

True connection transcends this physical plane, delving into the emotional, even spiritual, cores of our beings. It describes a bond forged from a shared experience, vulnerable honesty, deep understanding, and mutual respect. These connections satisfy a basic human craving for empathy – a sense of belonging and appreciation. When you share a genuine connection with a person, you feel seen, heard, and valued for who you truly are.

2.2. Importance of Emotional Resonance

Emotional resonance lies at the heart of deep and meaningful connections. It entails a shared emotional wavelength, a mutual understanding that goes beyond verbally expressed ideas. This kind of connection gives birth to a sense of trust, empathy, and comfort. When you feel that someone genuinely understands you, you lower your defenses, opening up new layers of your personality. In turn, this makes the connection even deeper, continuing a positive feedback cycle of deepening mutual understanding.

It isn't necessary for you both to agree on everything or share identical hobbies. Emotional resonance occurs when you align in your core values, ethics, and outlooks towards life. It's okay to have your unique interests - these differences can complement and enhance your connection. At the end of the day, it's about accepting each other exactly as you are.

2.3. Understanding and Trust: The Pillars of Connection

Understanding and trust are the vital pillars on which any connection rests. Seeking to understand before being understood is a mantra borrowed from Stephen Covey's "7 Habits of Highly Effective People." Why is this mantra crucial? Because it places the onus of understanding onto you. It requires you to approach situations and conversations with an open mind, a willingness to truly listen, and learn from the other person.

Trust is an extension of understanding. It's built over time, reinforced every time you keep a promise - when you stand by the other person in their time of need, remain respectful of their boundaries, and share both joy and sorrow. Trust is not given overnight, and once broken can be challenging to repair. However, an honest conversation acknowledging errors and willingness to change can mend broken trust and strengthen the bond.

2.4. Communication: The Bridge of Connection

Once the pillars of understanding and trust are in place, effective communication acts as a bridge that connects two individuals. Merely using the right words doesn't constitute effective communication. It's about empathy, actively listening, observing non-verbal cues, and acknowledging the other person's feelings.

An integral part of this process is feedback. Avoiding assumptions and clarifying misunderstandings can save relationships from needless turmoil. Constructive feedback, given with kindness and understanding, aids in the growth of both individuals and the relationship.

2.5. Cultivating Self-awareness

Self-awareness is an often overlooked, but crucial aspect of building connections. Understanding your emotions, strengths, weaknesses, and triggers can significantly impact how you perceive and interact with others. When you are self-aware, you can communicate more authentically, align your actions with your values, and manage your emotions effectively. This authenticity not only builds trust but also encourages the other person to be genuine, further strengthening the bond.

True connection is a journey, a continuous process of learning, growing, and sharing. It requires time, patience, and effort, but the reward is a fulfilling relationship that enriches your life. Through genuine connection, you truly comprehend the joy of being human –

with shared experiences, mutual growth, and an understanding that binds us together through thick and thin. Meanwhile, remember, the person you need to connect with the most is yourself. Without self-love and understanding, connecting with others becomes a challenge. Your journey to true connection, thus, begins with you.

Chapter 3. Cracking the Code of Communication

The beauty of human connection lies in understanding and being understood. This synergy is best achieved through adept communication, a skill we're about to explore in-depth in this chapter. While the process may seem daunting, let's remember communication is not an elitist art but a human need, a shared language meant to bring us closer together.

3.1. The Essence of Communication

Communication, in its most basic sense, is the process through which we exchange information and share meaning. It's not only about speaking and listening. It incorporates our body language, tone of voice, timing, and even silence. Whether we are aware of it or not, we are continually engaged in different forms of communication.

Verbal content is just the top of the iceberg. Beneath the waterline, hidden from sight but carrying extensive weight, are non-verbal cues and context. Non-verbal communication, such as eye contact, gestures, facial expression, touch, and body alignment, often carries more weight than words. It forms the undercurrent of our interactions and bridges the gap where words fall short, enabling us to understand each other beyond spoken language.

3.2. Grasping the Power of Listening

Listening is the usually underappreciated half of communication. However, becoming a better listener can often transform the quality of your relationships more than any other single practice. It's more than being silent when another person speaks; it's engaging and showing a genuine interest. It's about transferring the message from the voice of the speaker to the understanding of the listener.

Active listening involves making conscious efforts to really hear what the other person is saying and respond appropriately. It's characterized by maintaining eye contact, nodding when in agreement, and asking probing questions for heightened clarity. Active listening is an art, allowing you to get to the heart of the other person's feelings and thought processes.

3.3. The Power of Empathy in Communication

Empathy's role in fostering better communication cannot be overestimated. It's an ability to "walk in someone else's shoes" and understand their feelings and perspectives. Empathic communication means maintaining an understanding and compassionate stance during interactions.

At its essence, empathic communication is about being present. It involves truly hearing the other person and responding from a place of understanding and awareness. It's not about solving their problem for you; it's about letting them know that they're not alone in solving it for themselves.

3.4. Articulating Your Thoughts Effectively

Articulating your thoughts effectively is an integral aspect of communication. To be articulate means to express oneself clearly and expressively. It involves conveying your thoughts in a way that others can easily understand, and it's a valuable skill to enhance.

Effective articulation starts with a clear understanding of your thoughts. It requires thinking before speaking, understanding the effects of your words, and considering how your communication will be received. It is best achieved by being concise, specific, audience-sensitive, and using a pleasant tone.

3.5. Handling Difficult Conversations

Difficult conversations are a part and parcel of human interaction. Having the ability to navigate them effectively is integral to building stronger relationships and reducing misunderstandings. These conversations differ from usual ones in the way they trigger our defenses, making us more likely to react rather than respond thoughtfully.

Key to handling these interactions is maintaining emotional balance and demonstrating respect for the other person's point of view. The ultimate aim here isn't winning the argument, but nurturing adaptability, co-operating together, and growing through the challenges at hand.

3.6. The Role of Feedback in Communication

Feedback in communication serves as course correction, helping align the sender's intended message and the receiver's perceived message. Constructive feedback promotes a better understanding between communicating parties, keeping channels open and dynamic.

The therapeutic power of feedback lies in its ability to bridge the comprehension gap and nurture continual growth. But it requires being sensitive to timing, phrasing words sensitively, focusing on the issue, and providing helpful suggestions for action.

Mastering the art of effective communication is more than just sharing information; it is about understanding the emotions and intentions behind that information. Beyond enhancing your personal relationships, better communication skills can lead to improved interactions in every aspect of life. As we explore the nooks and crannies of these elements in subsequent pages, you'll discover how improving communication can transform your life one conversation at a time.

Chapter 4. The Art of Active Listening

In the realm of meaningful communication, practicing active listening is a key aspect. Its importance stems from the fact that we spend a vast amount of our lives listening - to our coworkers, families, friends, and other meaningful elements in our lives. Despite this, many of us have never had formal training in the skill. It's time to delve into the art of active listening, to understand its real essence and enrich our daily interactions.

4.1. The Concept of Active Listening

Active listening is not merely hearing the words that are spoken by another person. It involves attentiveness, empathetic response, and confirmation of understanding the speaker's message. It is the full engagement in the process of receiving, perceiving, and reacting to the information exchanged, ultimately deepening our relationships.

Peter Drucker, a renowned management consultant, emphasized that "the most important thing in communication is to hear what isn't being said." Thus, active listening also involves picking up non-verbal cues. Understanding the essence of these unvoiced messages allows us to grasp the complete picture the speaker is portraying.

Active listening brings numerous rewards such as building trust, fostering a stronger bond, resolving conflicts, and ensuring mutual understanding in communication. To make active listening more approachable, we need to familiarize ourselves with its techniques and methods and practice them until they become our second nature.

4.2. The Techniques of Active Listening

Active listening involves several techniques that can be implemented in your day-to-day communication. These include:

- **Encouragement**: Visual and verbal cues such as nodding, maintaining eye contact, or simple 'uh-huh's help the speaker know that you're paying attention, encouraging them to continue their discourse.

- **Clarification**: It involves asking questions or requesting more information to ensure clarity and understanding of the speaker's message.

- **Reflection**: Make an effort to reflect or mirror the speaker's feelings and ideas. This not only shows understanding but also assures the speaker that their feelings are valid.

- **Empathetic statements**: Displaying understanding of the speaker's feelings and situation can help bridge gaps in communication, providing a safe space for the conversation.

Furthermore, active listening isn't about interrupting or preparing for your turn to speak, it's about understanding another's perspective before sharing your own. It's crucial to avoid distractions and stay focused on the dialogue.

4.3. Importance of Body Language in Active Listening

Non-verbal communication is a vital component of active listening. It includes posture, facial expressions, gestures, and eye contact. To demonstrate engagement without using words, you can:

- Maintain an open body posture, facing the speaker directly.

- Lean slightly towards the speaker, conveying your interest.

- Nod your head in understanding.

- Maintain consistent eye contact without staring to show respect and interest.

Remember, body language can often reflect your unspoken sentiments. Therefore, keeping it consistent with your verbal responses is vital in making the speaker comfortable and fostering openness in conversation.

4.4. Overcoming the Barriers of Active Listening

There might be inner or outer barriers obstructing your attempts to listen actively. These may include:

- **Being judgmental**: It's important to keep an open mind and avoid negative assumptions about the speaker.

- **Interrupting the speaker**: Interrupting the conversation prohibits the full expression of thoughts, thereby hindering the process of active listening.

- **Distractions**: Eliminate exterior distractions like a television, cellphone, or loud noises as much as possible to keep attention focused.

Facing such barriers, it's crucial to remember that active listening is a skill that, like any other, can be improved with practice, persistence, and the right mindset.

4.5. Aiding Active Listening with Mindfulness

Mindfulness refers to the ability to stay focused on the present moment. When brought into our listening habits, mindfulness greatly enhances our capacity to fully comprehend and engage with the spoken word. Practicing mindfulness includes:

- Focusing entirely on the speaker and their words.

- Letting go of the desire to reply immediately.

- Avoiding distractions and staying in the moment.

Incorporating mindfulness not only helps in active listening but also improves overall communication, helping cultivate more significant relationships.

4.6. The Power of Silence in Active Listening

Active listening is not about constant interaction - silence, too, plays a crucial role. A well-timed pause allows both the speaker and listener to process information, formulating thoughtful responses. Indeed, silence often encourages more profound sharing, fostering deeper understanding and connection.

Silence should not be interpreted as disinterest, quite the contrary. It shows the listener is respecting the speaker's time to express themselves fully. Therefore, embracing silence as an integral part of active listening can lead to more insightful conversations.

4.7. Active Listening in Different Contexts

The application of active listening varies slightly depending on the context, such as in personal relationships, workplaces, or therapeutic environments. Each requires a unique blend of techniques grounded in the main principles of active listening.

In conclusion, mastering the art of active listening can be challenging, but the rewards are worthwhile. Not only does it change how we communicate, but it also profoundly affects our relationships with others. Let's venture into this journey of enhancing our listening skills and reaping its benefits in every walk of life. Understanding the other, rather than winning an argument, could indeed mark the beginning of building meaningful relationships through better communication.

Chapter 5. Bridging the Gap: Empathy in Communication

Communication is the lifeblood of human relationships, yet in an era defined by digital interaction, expressiveness and understanding are often lost. We frequently misunderstand each other due to lack of facial cues or voice tonality, and in the process, feel disconnected. A remedy to this growing issue, empathy marks the difference between simple communication and true connection.

5.1. Understanding Empathy

Empathy is the ability to understand and share the feelings of another. It's about seeing the world through their lens, enabling a deeper connection. Empathy isn't about fixing someone's problems, but about understanding them, giving them the space they need, and assuring them they're not alone.

To enhance our relationships, we have to put ourselves in the shoes of others. This doesn't mean losing sight of our viewpoint; it means broadening our perspective to encompass theirs. Empathy leads to richer, more authentic connections, bridges gaps of misunderstanding, and propagates an environment of nurturing growth and support.

5.2. The Practice of Empathy

Practicing empathy begins with active listening. When we engage completely in a conversation, we open doors to a deeper level of connection. To achieve this, focus on understanding the speaker's perspective without planning your response simultaneously. Validate their feelings and express your understanding by summarizing what you understood in your words.

Active listening doesn't end after the conversation. Reflecting on the discussion also contributes to understanding their perspective. Think about their expressions, revisit their words, infer hidden meanings, and comprehend what was left unsaid.

Let's dive into some strategies to practice empathy in communication more effectively:

1. Sensitivity to Non-Verbal Cues: Facial expressions, body language, and tone of voice often express more than words. A true empath will be in tune with these subtle signals.

2. Emotional Awareness: Sensitizing ourselves to our emotions helps us identify similar feelings in others. Be mindful of your feelings and the emotions that others evoke in you.

3. Patience and Open-mindedness: Preconceived notions and biases can obstruct understanding. Patience and open-mindedness strip away these barriers, permitting raw empathy.

5.3. Empathy Vs. Sympathy

Despite being closely related, empathy and sympathy aren't interchangeable. Sympathy is feeling compassion or sadness for someone's misfortune, an external perspective. Empathy, altogether different, involves sharing the feelings, an internal perspective.

The distinction between them is imperative to effective communication. While sympathy often keeps the focus on you, empathy redirects that focus on the other person, fostering a deeper connection.

5.4. Empathy in Everyday Communication

Daily life provides numerous opportunities to practice empathy. Each interaction, whether with colleagues, friends, family, or strangers, offers a chance to understand different perspectives. Be it a heated debate or a casual chat, empathy can transform the dynamics of dialogue.

When disagreements spark - a commonplace in human interaction - empathy can deescalate the situation. Projecting ourselves onto their viewpoint can expose another facet of truth which we may have overlooked. A collective truth emerges when we weave together their perspective with ours.

5.5. Gaining Deeper Relationships Through Empathy

Empathy is a bridge over the gaps of misunderstanding, a tool to mend tattered communication, and a means towards profound bonding. When we understand, acknowledge, and reciprocate the feelings of others, we establish a foundation for a nurturing relationship.

However, it's essential to remember that empathy isn't about self-sacrifice. It's generously giving without draining oneself. It's essential to maintain a balance, take care of our mental health, while assisting others on their emotional journeys.

As we journey through life, we interact with a myriad of perspectives. By practicing empathy, we can enrich those interactions, building deeper, healthier relationships. A labyrinth of communication unraveling, offering treasures of profound connection and fulfillment. Let's step into this labyrinth, let's bridge the gap with the cornerstone of empathetic communication.

Chapter 6. Non-Verbal Cues: The Unspoken Language

Communication extends far beyond the spoken or written word. Over half of our communication occurs through non-verbal cues - a 'silent' language that can sometimes speak louder than words.

6.1. The Importance of Non-Verbal Communication

Across different cultures and languages, many non-verbal cues remain universally understood. A smile can signal friendship, while a furrowed brow might signify displeasure. In this way, non-verbal signals become a crucial part of how we understand each other, especially when words fail us.

Whether conscious or unconscious, these signals portray our feelings and attitudes, often more accurately than our words. They bring a level of authenticity to our messages, impossible to convey through verbal means alone. Consequently, understanding non-verbal cues leads to a deeper and more meaningful connection with others, by offering insight into their emotions and thoughts.

6.2. Observing Non-Verbal Cues

Though the importance of non-verbal communication is clear, learning to read these signals accurately can be complex. They can often be subtle, fleeting, and dependent on context.

Various facets reflect non-verbal communication - facial expressions, body language, gestures, eye contact, touch, and even space.

Facial expressions are potent indicators of emotions. They can hint at feelings of happiness, sadness, anger, surprise, fear, and disgust. Despite cultural differences, these basic emotions are universally recognized through facial expressions.

Body language and posture share numerous insights about a person's state of mind. An approachable person might stand with an open posture, with arms relaxed and feet shoulder-width apart. Meanwhile, crossed arms could denote defensibility or discomfort.

Gestures, though often subconscious, can express a range of feelings and attitudes. A thumbs-up might indicate approval, while a shrug may show uncertainty or indifference.

Eye contact is a powerful non-verbal cue. It signals various emotions and reactions like interest, affection, hostility, or attraction. It's a key component in maintaining engagement in a conversation and showing that we're attentive and respectful.

The use of touch or haptics is another form of non-verbal communication. An encouraging pat on the back, a warm hug, or a supportive touch on the arm can convey feelings of care, comfort, or encouragement.

Spatial relations or proxemics reveal a lot about relationships and reactions. For example, standing or sitting close to someone often indicates intimacy or comfort, while maintaining a greater distance may suggest formality or discomfort.

But remember! No single non-verbal cue tells the full story. Always consider the combination of signals and the given context for a more accurate interpretation.

6.3. Enhancing Communication through Non-Verbal Cues

Understanding the basics of non-verbal communication allows us to take a more conscious approach to our interactions.

Conveying the correct non-verbal cues can enhance the effectiveness of our communication. Consistency between verbal and non-verbal communication heightens trust and fosters a connection.

However, mismatched verbal and non-verbal messages can create confusion or mistrust. For example, if you say you're happy while frowning, your listener will likely trust your facial expression more than your words.

Also, being aware of the other person's non-verbal cues can elevate your empathy and understanding, improving the quality of your relationships.

6.4. The Role of Culture in Non-Verbal Communication

A note of caution, however. Culture significantly affects non-verbal communication. A gesture that is harmless in one culture can be offensive in another. Therefore, understanding cultural differences is crucial when interpreting non-verbal cues accurately.

One must consider cultural norms, respect them, and avoid stereotyping based on an individual's non-verbal cues.

Your journey to mastering the art of non-verbal communication starts here. Remember, it's not about perfect execution but about growing awareness and understanding. This key offers a path to enriched relationships and a true connection that spans beyond words. Allow this unspoken language to reveal the full depth of your compassion, openness, and ability to resonate with others. Hence, letting your relationships blossom in a more heartwarming and profound manner than ever before.

Chapter 7. The Power of Positive Communication

Every great idea, every sincere expression of affection, and every impactful decision begin with communication. This indispensable tool, which seems simple on the surface, has an innate power to carry love, bring smiles, resolve conflicts, usher understanding, and even alter destineties. Positive communication signifies using this universally potent tool in the best way possible. It pushes us towards a state where every interpersonal interaction is a nourishing experience, an exploration of our shared values, beliefs and potential.

7.1. A Close Look at Positive Communication

Positive communication isn't just about using respectful language or being nice. It's much deeper than that. It represents a mindset, a certain attitude, a quality of intention that encapsulates honesty, consideration, and empathy. The essence of positive communication is to convey information, ideas, or feelings in a way that they are heard, understood, taken seriously, and duly responded to. The focus is not just on the content of the message but also on the process of communication. It grants importance to not just what is being said, but also how it is being said.

The salient components of positive communication involve non-verbal cues such as maintaining eye contact, appropriate body gestures, tone of voice, and active engagement during the conversation. All these elements play a crucial role in creating an environment where positive interactions can flourish.

7.2. Influencing Relationships

Positive communication dramatically influences the nature and quality of relationships around us. How we interact with people defines how they perceive us, and consequently how they respond to our needs and wants.

Take, for instance, a professional environment. When employees feel heard, understood and respected through positive communication, the workplace becomes a breeding ground for creativity and productivity. The employees are motivated, there's a sense of belonging, and a supportive environment, fostering not just individual growth but promoting overall organizational development too.

Similarly, in personal relationships, positive communication leads to stronger bonds. When we approach our friends, family, or loved ones with positive communication, we create a space of transparency, trust, and mutual respect. It fosters the understanding that binds people together and allows for a deeper, more meaningful connection.

7.3. The Techniques of Positive Communication

How can we embed the concept of positive communication into our daily interactions? Here are some of the widely accepted and effective techniques:

1. Open-ended Questions: Ask questions that can't be answered by a simple 'yes' or 'no'. Encourage the other person to express their opinion or feelings, showcasing interest and empathy.

2. Active Listening: Give your full attention to the communicator. Show an understanding by asking clarifying questions,

summarizing, or paraphrasing what you have heard, reinforcing the person's value and importance.

3. Offering Validations: Acknowledge the other person's thoughts, feelings, and experiences. You don't have to agree necessarily, but a simple validation shows that you value their perspective.

4. Use Non-verbal Signals: Maintain eye contact, lean in, and use facial expressions and body language that show you are receptive and engaged in the conversation.

5. Assertive Communication: Speak your mind clearly and respectfully without undermining the rights and views of others.

7.4. The Impacts of Positive Communication

Once you start applying these techniques of positive communication, you will witness a substantial positive change in your surroundings. Whether it's your workplace or your home, people will respond more positively, conflicts would resolve more peacefully, ideas will be shared more openly, and relationships will feel more fulfilling.

The significance is particularly pronounced in conflict situations. Disputes can be an opportunity for growth and better understanding if dealt with positive communication. They cease to be a test of who's winning, instead, they become a platform for exploring possibilities, negotiating, and finding common ground.

7.5. Conclusion

Positive communication is a powerful expedient to build and nurture relationships. It steps beyond mere words and explores the profound subtleties that can bring about a profound difference in our interactions, our relationships, and our lives. By consciously incorporating aspects of positive communication into our daily interactions, we open ourselves up to more meaningful connections, richer understanding, and a more fulfilling life.

A journey towards positive communication is essentially a journey towards empathy, understanding, and authenticity, values which remain at the heart of strong, healthy relationships. Embrace this transformative power, enrich your interactions and enliven your relationships, leading towards happiness, fulfillment, and growth, at both personal and collective levels.

The power of positive communication is truly limitless, facilitating a human connection that is deeper than language, and transcends any barrier. Become the change agent in your life, choose to communicate positively and experience the remarkable transformation it brings.

Chapter 8. Managing Conflicts through Constructive Dialogues

Conflict is an inevitable part of human relationships. Whether you engage in conversations with a life partner, a business associate, a peer, or a friend, differences of opinion are bound to surface. How we manage these differences, these 'conflicts,' determines the strength and longevity of our relationships. This chapter explores how constructive dialogues can mold conflict into an opportunity for growth, understanding, and further connection.

8.1. The Phenomenon of Conflict

To effectively manage conflict, we first need to understand what it is - and, perhaps crucially, what it is not. Contrary to popular belief, conflict is not inherently destructive or negative. Conflict arises when there is a gap between what we expect and what we experience, a discrepancy between what we want and what we get. It's a signal that change is required.

The key is not to avoid conflict but to approach it constructively. And the first step in that direction is understanding our perception of conflict. Many people dread conflict, viewing it as a threat, an argument, or a sign of trouble. Instead, try to perceive conflict as an opportunity — an invitation for conversation, an opening for deeper understanding, and a catalyst for growth.

8.2. Understanding Constructive Dialogues

A constructive dialogue is not simply a polished debate; it is an interaction where participants aim to understand, learn, and grow together rather than trying to win an argument. It's an exchange of perspectives where the heart listens as much as the mind, and new shared meanings are created.

In constructive dialogues, differences are not seen as threats but potentials for innovation and mutual growth. Instead of homing in on the 'right' or the 'wrong,' emphasis is given on understanding 'why' and 'how.' Such a conversation agenda transforms the talking table into a learning platform and aligns individual paradigms towards a shared reality.

8.3. The Essential Steps to Constructive Dialogues

This does not mean that moving towards constructive dialogues is easy. It requires patience, practice, and a methodical approach. Here we outline the steps to a successful, constructive dialogue.

1. Preparedness: Before you initiate the dialogue, gather your thoughts. Identify your feelings and understand why you feel that way. Review the issue from a broader perspective, and be clear on what you want to communicate.

2. Invitation: Set the stage for conversation. A non-threatening invitation that expresses your feelings and readiness to understand theirs can work wonders. Show respect and make sure your partner also feels prepared to engage.

3. Active Listening: Once the conversation begins, ensure to listen as much as, if not more than, you speak. Try to comprehend their

viewpoint completely. Ask clarifying questions, but refrain from interrogation.

4. Expressing: Clearly express your feelings and perspective. Be honest, but tactful. Use 'I' statements to avoid inadvertent blame.

5. Sympathizing: Acknowledge their feelings and show empathy. Validation does not necessarily mean agreement; you can understand someone's feelings without accepting their viewpoint completely.

6. Collaborating: Work together to find a solution or agreement. Remember, the goal here is not to win, but to resolve.

8.4. Emotional Intelligence and Constructive Dialogues

Emotional intelligence plays an integral part in constructive dialogues. Not only does it aid in understanding and expressing emotions effectively, but it also helps manage the tension in the air during conflicts.

Keeping your emotions in check, showing empathy, and navigating the conversation without flaring up requires emotional intelligence. It enables you to manage your emotional reactions, think clearly, make sound decisions, and maintain a constructive dialogue even in heat. By practicing emotional intelligence, you pave the way for conversations that enrich relationships, not strain them.

8.5. Patience: A Quintessential Ingredient

Patience is a crucial factor behind successful constructive dialogues. Relationships cannot change overnight, and neither can practices. Being patient with yourself and others during this process is essential. Understand that mistakes will be made, and old habits may creep in, but with time, change will arrive.

8.6. Conclusion: Turning Conflicts into Opportunities

Conflict need not be a dreaded word. With the right skills and heart-set, these can be turned into opportunities for growth and bonding. By adopting constructive dialogues, conflicts become less about winning and more about understanding, less about defending and more about connecting. Your relationships start transforming, becoming a platform of shared truths, empathy, respect, and mutual growth.

Through these guidelines, this chapter has given you steps to embrace conflict not as a dreaded confrontation but as an opportunity; the opportunity to truly connect, communicate, and enhance your relationships. The journey may be challenging, but the outcomes – profound relationships, deeper understanding, personal growth – are truly enriching.

Chapter 9. Relationship Building: One Conversation at a Time

Imagine going to bed each night feeling fulfilled, supported, and understood. Picture waking up each morning to a world where every interaction you have is filled with respect, compassion, and genuine connection. This perhaps sounds far-fetched in a world teetering more toward disconnection, but it doesn't have to be. It begins with just one conversation at a time.

9.1. The Power of Genuine Conversations

When we refer to genuine conversations, we're not merely talking about the exchange of words. It's about expressing our thoughts, emotions, beliefs - our soul's language, with honesty and openness. It means engaging in a dialogue where both parties are willing and ready to intervene, listen, understand and respond without judgement.

Each conversation is an opportunity to foster trust, empathy, and mutual respect — to improve our relationships and life quality. The real transformation begins when we reconsider the impact a single conversation can make.

Let's dissect a simple conversation. There are three main components: the speaker, the listener, and the message. These hold the potential for establishing a true connection, and in the following sections we will delve into strategies to amplify each component's effectiveness.

9.2. Speaking with Intentii

The art of conversation starts with you, the speaker. Speaking with intentions implies that each word you utter carries a purpose, it is neither random nor spontaneous. This purpose might be to convey information, share emotions, or seek support. By adopting intentional speaking, you invite meaningful conversations into your life.

To speak with intent, strive for clarity and honesty in your messages. Be explicit about your needs, desires, and feelings using 'I' statements, such as "I feel" or "I prefer". Avoid blame or judgement to preserve the space where relationships can foster.

Remember, speaking isn't solely about being heard – it's about being understood. Adjust your communication style based on the listener. To do so, consider their background, perspective, and current emotional state. This not only facilitates comprehension but demonstrates respect for your conversation partner.

9.3. Active Listening: A Gift of Presence

Active listening extends beyond hearing the spoken words. It demands presence, empathy, and an understanding heart. It's about validating feelings, providing empathy, and maintaining an open mind.

This might mean removing distractions, maintaining eye contact, or providing soft affirmations to acknowledge the speaker. It also includes non-verbal cues like nods or a comforting touch. Reflective statements, summarizing or paraphrasing the speaker's words, can signify your understanding while offering the speaker a chance to clarify if needed.

Remember, active listening isn't about offering solutions or fixing problems (unless explicitly asked for). It's about providing a safe space for the speaker to express themselves freely, feel understood, and valued.

9.4. The Art of Non-Verbal Communication

Non-verbal cues significantly impact the tone and outcomes of conversations. They can reinforce or contradict our words. Understanding them can elevate your communication game.

These cues include facial expressions, body language, tone of voice, gestures, and physical distance. The key isn't necessarily to master reading them, but to start paying more attention. Observe whether the speaker's words align with their cues. If there's a discrepancy, offer an open-ended question, like "You say you're fine, but you look troubled. Is there anything you want to talk about?"

9.5. The Language of Empathy

Empathy plays an indispensable role in relationship building. It's the ability to understand and share the feelings of others. To empathize is to step into another's shoes, view the world from their perspective and respond with care.

Many mistakenly view empathy as agreeing or identifying with the feelings of the speaker. But empathy doesn't require agreement - it seeks understanding. It's the bridge that connects hearts, fosters trust, and turns ordinary conversations into extraordinary bonding experiences.

9.6. Difficult Conversations & Conflict Resolution

No relationship is devoid of conflict. Misunderstandings, disagreements, and miscommunications are part of the human dynamics. However, these 'difficult' conversations, if handled correctly, can be a catalyst for relationship growth.

In handling difficult conversations, follow these steps:

1. Preparation: Understand your feelings and needs before entering the conversation.

2. Execution: Use 'I' statements, express your feelings and needs, respectfully hear the other party out.

3. Resolution: Find a mutually agreeable solution without compromising your needs.

Mastery over these steps requires time, patience, and continual practice. While challenging at first, their habitual use can revitalize your relationships.

9.7. Self-Reflection and Continuous Learning

Your conversation journey doesn't end here. Treat each conversation as a learning opportunity. Reflect on what went well and what could be improved. Consider both perspectives.

Growing as a communicator is a continuous process. Appreciate your efforts and the progress you make, no matter how small. Gradually, you will realize that this journey of building relationships one conversation at a time is life-changing.

Remember, your voice matters, your feelings matter, and your relationships matter. Treasure each conversation, for it carries the potential not only to build relationships but to transform lives, including your own.

35

Chapter 10. Leaning into Difficult Conversations

In an ever-diversifying world, we regularly encounter situations that require tough conversations. They may be with loved ones, teammates, bosses, colleagues, or even ourselves. These conversations are an inevitable part of our relational lives. They can be charged with emotional intensity often leading to discomfort, but they are essential. They possess the potential to increase understanding, build trust, and foster deeper personal and professional relationships. Often, people tend to avoid difficult conversations, as the stakes are high, emotions run strong, and there are multiple viewpoints. However, the ability to handle such conversations is a vital skill in forging stronger, more honest, and direct relationships.

10.1. Understanding the Importance of Difficult Conversations

Difficult conversations are not necessarily about confrontation or discord. They are about understanding and finding a common ground. When we open ourselves to these conversations and encounter the emotions they evoke, we open pathways to learning and collaboration. Tough conversations may address disagreements, miscommunications, confessions, or addressing behavior. They can be painful, but they offer valuable opportunities for individual and relational growth.

The avoidance of these conversations often leads to the buildup of resentment and unexpressed feelings, thus inhibiting authentic connection. On the contrary, embracing these conversations can lead to surprising levels of intimacy and trust. This understanding brings forth a need to lean into difficult conversations despite our hesitation.

10.2. Preparing for Difficult Conversations

Preparation is the first crucial step. Firstly, identify what the conversation is essentially about. Secondly, know what you hope to achieve by having this conversation. A clear understanding of your purpose helps in keeping the conversation focused and effective.

An essential part of the plan is to choose an appropriate time and place that is convenient for both parties. In choosing a place, ensure it sets a neutral and comfortable atmosphere.

You also need to consider the person you are engaging with. Understand their communication style and adjust yours in a way that conveys your message effectively yet empathetically. Every person has their unique way of processing information, so a receptive approach based on understanding helps steer the conversation in a positive direction.

Knowing the facts and having them at your fingertips is also vital. This proves useful especially when the conversation is about concrete issues that require factual clarity.

An often overlooked but crucial aspect of preparation is preparing oneself emotionally. The ability to remain calm can guide the conversation effectively, preventing it from becoming a battleground of reactive emotions.

10.3. Navigating Emotions During Difficult Conversations

Emotions are the heart of difficult conversations. They indicate that the topic at hand impacts us on a deeper level. Acknowledging our emotions helps clarify what's at stake and provides guiding insights. However, our emotions shouldn't overrun the conversation.

Be mindful of the other person's emotional state as well. Listening to their feelings and showing empathy can help in managing and steering the emotional terrain of the conversation.

The ability to detach oneself from any negative emotions is integral to maintaining composure. Doing so allows space for logical and empathetic thinking.

10.4. Communicating Effectively

Effective communication is not just about speaking; it's listening as well. Active listening is instrumental in understanding the other person's viewpoint and showing respect for their feelings.

Speak your truth but remember to employ empathy to ensure your words are not hurtful. Avoid accusatory language and instead use 'I' statements. This promotes an atmosphere of understanding rather than one of blame.

=== Dealing with Defensive Reactions

Defensiveness is a common reaction when individuals feel attacked or misunderstood. It turns a conversation into conflict. To ward off defensiveness, a non-aggressive and non-judgmental approach is essential.

If the other party becomes defensive, stop and reassess. Understand their perspective and reaffirm your intention of understanding rather than attacking. If you become defensive, recognize it, pause, and remind yourself of the primary purpose of the conversation.

=== Closing the Conversation Positively

Difficult conversations need not end negatively. You may not agree with the other party, but understanding and respect for each other's viewpoint should be reached. To maintain a positive end, revisit the key points succinctly, expressing gratitude for their time.

Remember that the primary goal of difficult conversations is not to win, but to foster understanding, empathy, and progress. After all, the quality of our lives frequently depends on the quality of our communications.

Leaning into difficult conversations may not be easy, but with the right strategies and empathy, it is one way to forge profound connections, promoting growth and development. By embracing these uncomfortable truths and challenging conversations, we build more meaningful relationships, fostering a deeper understanding of each other and ourselves.

Chapter 11. Communication and Connection: The Path Forward

Let's begin on a journey where we discover not just the act of communicating, but the art of creating a significant connection. Our first step is to understand and appreciate the profound bond between communication and connection in enlivening our relationships.

11.1. The Correlation between Connection and Communication

Communication lies at the heart of every significant human relationship. It is the process that enables us to relay information, thoughts, feelings, and ideas. While connection, on the other hand, relates to the sense of being in tune with another person. It's the underlying emotional bond that transcends mere information exchange, adding more depth and significance to a relationship.

In this web of human interactions, communication is the tool, and connection is the result. We use various forms of communication – spoken words, written text, body language, and numerous subtle cues to connect with one another on different levels. It's an inseparable dyad where the quality of our communication directly influences the depth of the connection we establish.

11.2. Unveiling the Layers of Communication

Communication is not merely an exchange of words; it runs deeper, spreading its roots into intellectual, emotional, and psychological aspects of our lives.

Intellectual Communication is the foundation and most prevalent form, dealing with the sharing of information, facts, and ideas. This layer is straightforward and predominantly logic-intensive.

Emotional Communication, however, works on a deeper plane, influencing our feelings and moods. It pertains to expressing our unique emotional states and empathetically understanding others.

Psychological Communication treads further into the realm of the subconscious, encompassing the subtle cues hidden in our tone, body language, and unexpressed thoughts affecting our interactions.

To truly connect with others, we need to become well-versed in all these layers, consciously combining them to create a meaningful dialogue.

11.3. Formulating the Matrix of Genuine Connection

A genuine connection is not formed overnight. It requires constant effort, conscious understanding, and an unwavering commitment to comprehend and validate another's experiences. Let's explore the crucial elements that build these bonds:

Empathy plays a central role in forging deeper connections. It's the ability to put ourselves in another's shoes completely, experiencing their emotions as our own.

Authenticity, being true to oneself, serves as the pillar for any genuine relationship. It's about communicating our thoughts, feelings, and vulnerabilities openly, without the veneer of pretension.

Respect is about valuing all forms of communication. Even though we may not agree with another's perspective, it's essential to respect their viewpoint and express our disagreement in a kind, empathetic manner.

Trust is one of the most potent forces in building connections. It's earned through consistent, honest, and open communication.

11.4. Improving Communication: Putting The Pieces Together

Building robust communication skills is a gradual process. Here are some strategies:

1. Be an Active Listener: Active listening isn't just about hearing; it's about attentive understanding with empathetic responses demonstrating that we value others' views.

2. Understand Non-Verbal Cues: Being aware of body language, tone, and facial expressions is crucial as these non-verbal cues often communicate more than words.

3. Practice Mindful Communication: Engage in conversations with presence, attentiveness, and intentionality. Keep distractions at bay and focus solely on the interaction at hand.

4. Keep an Open Mind: Avoid getting entrenched in biases or assumptions. They cloud our perspective and act as obstacles in genuine communication.

5. Maintain Transparency: Whether it's acknowledging a mistake or expressing gratitude, straightforwardness strengthens communication and consequently, connection.

11.5. From Communication to Connection: Your Path Ahead

The journey from communication to connection is unique for every individual; it's a path filled with understanding, empathy, authenticity, respect, and trust.

By consciously focusing on our communication—the way we convey our thoughts, how we interpret others, the phases where we falter, and when we thrive—we transform ordinary exchanges into profound experiences.

In the end, it's all about striving towards honesty— removing our protective armor, confronting our fears and insecurities, and embracing vulnerability. Defying the fear of being judged and willingly opening the door to our hearts, thus paving way for profound connections to flourish. This transformation will be unique and intimate, leading to a life enriched with meaningful relationships. Let's embark on this journey together, towards a world entrenched in the warmth of true human connection.